T0017216

Sowell Collection Books

SERIES EDITORS KURT CASWELL,
KRISTIN D. LOYD, DIANE WARNER

WATER

POEMS AND
DRAWINGS

SUSAN
BRIND
MORROW

TEXAS TECH UNIVERSITY PRESS

This book is typeset in Crimson Pro. The paper used in this
book meets the minimum requirements of ANSI/NISO
Z39.48-1992 (R1997). ♾

Designed by Hannah Gaskamp
Cover design by Hannah Gaskamp

Library of Congress Control Number: 2023942776

ISBN: 978-1-68283-183-0 (cloth)

Printed in the United States of America
23 24 25 26 27 28 29 30 31 / 9 8 7 6 5 4 3 2 1
Texas Tech University Press
Box 41037
Lubbock, Texas 79409-1037 USA
800.832.4042
ttup@ttu.edu
www.ttupress.org

CONTENTS

SERIES EDITORS' PREFACE

The book you now hold in your hands, *Water: Poems and Drawings* by Susan Brind Morrow, is the first publication of the Sowell Collection Books series, a new project in a family of projects that make up The Sowell Family Collection in Literature, Community, and the Natural World at Texas Tech University.

Founded in 1999, The Sowell Collection is a literary archive housing the papers of prominent twentieth and twenty-first century American writers whose work explores questions of land use and the environment, the nature of human and non-human communities, the intersection of scientific and spiritual values, and the fragility and resilience of the Earth. Writers whose papers are housed in The Sowell Collection have received many honors for literary and science writing, including the National Book Award, the MacArthur Fellowship, the Wallace Stegner Fellowship, and the John Burroughs Medal.

The community gathered around The Sowell Collection and its projects includes not only the writers whose papers make up the archive but the many students, teachers, writers, readers, researchers, archivists, librarians, and donors who have conducted research in the collection, participated in our conferences and reading series, and supported the collection in so many other ways.

The Sowell Collection Books series at Texas Tech University Press is an extension of this community, an invitation to join our conversation. The series publishes titles in any genre that centers on themes in alignment with those of the writers whose literary papers make up The Sowell Collection. Proposals and manuscripts are reviewed on an ongoing basis and may be directed to Texas Tech University Press.

Susan Brind Morrow, whose literary papers are housed in The Sowell Collection, is a classicist, memoirist, naturalist, and poet. While she is deeply rooted in the Finger Lakes region of upstate New York, she is also a wanderer. Much of her work stems from her travels in Egypt and the Sudan. Her writing captures the ephemerality, persistence, and beauty of the natural world.

In *Water: Poems and Drawings*, color is a defining principle of place. The interplay of light and shadow across a landscape reveals its truths, and water is ever present, even in its absence. The book is grounded in a sensory experience of the natural world. For Morrow, to know a place is to know it physically, tactilely, bodily. Language is also to be regarded bodily, as well as auricularly and visually. It is a medium through which to interpret and then to transmit the physical world from writer to reader.

Morrow delights in the multiplicities of language. She is a language hunter, a word collector. Her work lives in the liminal space between object and metaphor, that when engaged by a reader, reveals a profound reverence for mystery. Morrow's writing, then, is an act of seeking. Sometimes we know (or think we know) where she's taking us but are nevertheless surprised by where we end up.

We invite you to journey with Susan Brind Morrow's *Water*, and with us and our growing community.

KURT CASWELL, KRISTIN D. LOYD, AND DIANE WARNER
SERIES EDITORS

WATER

PART I

WATER

THE RADIANT LOVE THAT RECEIVES ALL PAIN

The grass is suited to the sea
Seaweed has the texture of skin
Something with rubbery round
Yellow leaves,
Razor grass reflects the sun,
All greens the colors of lichen
complement the sea.
Seed crowns flatten like wet straw
in the rain wind

Do you think the waves will hurt?
Hidden by spray they drown the thunder

FRESH WATER

Lake Superior is raised above the heart of this country like an angel's wing. Although it is an inland sea, its blue is not the cold steel blue of the ocean, but a kind of rich cornflower blue. As suddenly seen over the rim of a hill one cannot quite believe how vast this rich blue is, the largest expanse of fresh water on the planet Earth. In winter waves approach the shore and, unlike ocean waves, they freeze, into hard white mountains of flaking ice.

When I think of the lakes of my childhood, the Great Lakes, they conjure a sense of both sweetness and wildness at once. Beyond Chicago and Buffalo and Detroit, this territory of the great fresh water reserves of the world is for the most part unsettled, and unsought, like a secret treasure long ago forgotten. As Pindar wrote twenty-five hundred years ago, and as true today as it was then, *ariston men hudor*, the most precious thing is water/after that comes gold.

ḥȝwy
benighted traveler

ḥȝb
hippopotamus

ḥȝbȝs
starry sky

Stars rise bringing rain
And the earth to completion
In woven threads of blood
And summer grain

UPPER NILE

The land gave way. The river dispersed into winding streams through travelling fields of high papyrus, green and golden tufted in the sun. African water hyacinths, deep purple, soaking up light, and climbing vines of pale veiny flowers surrounded them. At night bright crowds of fireflies rose and fell through the dense screen of vegetation, doubled by their falling shadows, as we wound slowly on, stopping frequently because the depth was so low. The marsh could only remind me of the relief scenes at Saqqara that showed the Nile 4,000 years ago, the reeds filled with animals, sudden waterbirds surprised up from the thick undergrowth by hunters and their nets, a great primordial swamp where life begins, differs and proliferates out of control.

Coming away from the desert as I was, my sudden exposure to this world of plants made me believe that it was one of the strangest and most beautiful places on earth. The thickness of the scented air was intoxicating. There was no sense of prog-ress. Our path was obscured by varied sun-threaded greens that stretched to each horizon, swallowing the narrow lines of water every hundred yards.

Sitting up on the roof in the morning I would say to everyone around me, "*Ter da shinu?*" What is the name of that bird? and I had many different reports. The chestnut backed fish eagle and the tall goliath heron were our companions all the way. There were small black and white birds with streaming snakes-tongue tails three times the length of their bodies that spun circles behind them in flight, and bright insect-like bee-eaters the colors of precious stones.

SENECA LAKE

August 9th

It is the new moon.
The lake water is swollen up
in ocean waves.
Leaves beat the trees like paper.
The flag whips stiff against the air.
This is the earliest August
I remember:
A month of storms after drought
has taken down the birch leaves
and sucked the color
out of the ground

⁘

white
oak leaves
at Ross's

August 12th

Hazy, low, gray-bottomed clouds today. Still a cool wind, but

ZEITUN

I love to watch you walking in the evening
When you're afraid
And your wavering frame folds back arc-like
to fight the wind
Your skin melts golden with the sides of grass
And voices of birds skin
Your delicate heart.

yom yakun al nass zai farash mabthuthin
The day that people are scattered over the earth like moths

Millions of slender silver-winged insects
Swarming like pieces of silver
over the glass in the light

A pink sphinx,
A thick-horned moth with an owl's head
And now a creamy white one
speckled black
Like an emperor in ermine
Orange within
butts the silver insects
with its head
neuropteron translucent green
eyes ruby red

moths as though parading
moths like chips of gold
the scribbler
the Hebrew
the hieroglyph moth
the false geometer
pistachio emerald then
an electric blue one
that feeds only on irises
settles like dust on my hand

I can hear their wings
Clicking out of the dark

Not such were his strength and stout heart
The one I heard about from the old men talking
Who said they saw him break the ranks
Of Lydian Calvary on the Hermian plain,
The man with the white-ashen spear.

And Athena never blamed him at all
For the bitter anger in his heart
As he ran among the bloody thick of battle.
There was no one like him among all the people
For he moved like the rays of the sun.

THAW

Black earth, wet earth, first smell of spring.
We walk around the lake where the smashed ice
lies in loose low heaps like scree,
where the lake, refrozen now, broke and spilled
it in the wind. Our feet slide beneath us
in the steel grey evening. A mallard shot open spreads its
frozen insides on the ice—
thick and red around its waxy yellow organs
rimmed with iridescent feathers, blue and green,
a scrap thrown up—a treasure
of the splintering thaw

SWAMP

Hipboots on we wade through the swamp,
through sinkholes loose with peatmoss
and around peeled stumps gnawed down
by beaver into small uneven crests above the water.
All the colors of the autumn sun are here.
This was once a maple grove
and under the water
small pliant strands shoot up from the dead wood
with melon-colored hand-like leaves on them.

Bob rifles through his pockets for a granola bar
and hands me half. There are other hunters nearby.
We can hear how clumsy they are
and fear they'll frighten anything that comes away,
or shoot at us.

The sun drops in a shroud of light
through layers of pressed blue cloud
as strands of silver surface in the east.
We row away over the pond.
Though having shot nothing we are happy,
out in the cold air, aware of decay and change, woodsmoke
from chimneys, damp dying leaves.
Fields of dead corn stand dry by the roadside,
soon to be cornflakes, Bob says.

COLOR IN THE BAHAMAS

blue plum-bottomed clouds
stacked up high and gleaming
over the smooth water

the leaves of the palm
made spears of light
rattle in the wind

(that leaves open
out from the heart)

inca doves with rust red wings
and necks ringed black like tree bark

the birds darting in the coral garden
can they have been made for anything but decoration

the metal-green hummingbird in the hibiscus
the pale, streaked anole that eats a fallen crumb of cheese

the bleached coral
about which is thin red soil
enough for a grapefruit tree, lime tree
monkey fiddle, paw paw

all in the lemon-colored light of late evening
until the clouds blot it away

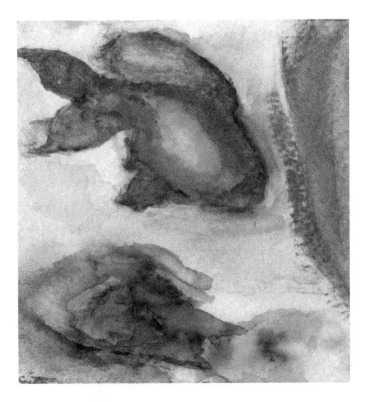

Spring comes with a rush of fresh water light

φαλλαινα, φαλος, φαλεριαω, φαλεριοντα

phallaina— a whale
phalos— (phaw)- shining white (phos, light, a human being)
phaleriaw— to be patched with white
phalerionta— waves crested with white foam

κελαδος, κελαινεφες, πεδιον κελαινεφεν

kelados— a noise of rushing waters; a loud clear voice; music
kelainephes— black with clouds, shrouded in dark clouds
pedion kelainephen— black, rich soil

THE SILVER FOREST

In the silver forest
the light is silver
and the hard leaves
of salt-fed trees
clatter in the wind
and the snakes and birds
in them
are invisible.
Their roots wind
through pocked iron coral
that on the surface
cuts like teeth,
roots carved in claws
as smooth and hard as ivory.
•
For a day I pretend
I am a creature of the sea.
I lay flat on the sand and let
the froth slide under me.

hush
no time
the waves are circular with
the tide

The leaves of the seaside
trees are silver
like the poplars beside Lake
Ontario,
beside Odysseus and
Nausicaa
the brown back

the leather hand
the ribbed sea sand.
Under the poplar trees
we have sherry and swim
in the deep blue water.
The poplar trees rattle in the
wind
as though there were ghosts
in them.

Under the water, where
weeds don't grow,
the sand is thick and ridged
and white—
delicious (the toes and lips
are confused).
The wind animates the
mineral earth
as though it were its disem-
bodied breath
this is a secret.

The sand lies down under
the waves
 the color of his skin,
and the water is the color of
my brother's eyes—here he
comes over the sand,
a mirror of me.
I close my eyes and have one
true friend.

ELBA

Thy mother is like a vine in thy blood planted by the waters, but now she is in the wilderness in a dry and thirsty ground

Gebel Elba

In the desert the coolness of the dark is the coolness of water. The hieroglyph for woman is a vessel of water, the holy grail.

Grey marguerites
In a prison of flowers
The petals pale silently down,
Right below, drown
on the bare ground
where a blond girl lies

Recall
Nothing in this world can match
The natural beauty of women
As they ripen to fullness
The good falls on her face
Her hand curls, veins blue
beside her swollen face
(We only inhabit these bodies.
A cold wind brings us home)
The wind strips the trees
freeing the leaves

GRAY MAGNOLIAS

In a prison of flowers
The petals fall steadily down
Thick and rotting, brown
On the bare ground
Where a blonde girl lies reading.

Nothing in this world can match
The natural beauty of women
As they ripen to fullness.

(We only inhabit these bodies.
A cold wind brings me home.)
The wind strips the trees,
Freeing the leaves.

MAHAS

Beautiful blue-lipped Sudanese, carrying child,
Stands sheathed in brown silk
                          with circular creases,
With Amazon eyes and a white wall of teeth while
The stagnant world falls limp around her shoulders.

Vertical scars retreat in war-drawn bows that frame her smile
And streams of soft-echoing sound follow her small rounded
feet

Hollyhocks that grow wild
in the desert

ANDROMEDA

The dragon has breasts
And the alabaster woman
Was chained by the warrior with wings
Who won her with his sword in the water
When she was wild

Now the beast waits to be taken
Skinned and diminished
Pathetically white
Whose beauty is betrayal
And utter helplessness
In the golden evening light

PYASA

In spring the apples in the untouched garden
of maidens are watered by flowing streams
and the tender vines grow
in the dark shade of the leaves.

But for me love has no season.
When the cold north wind
Bristles with lightning
Unstoppable and free
The parching madness of desire
Shakes my whole body

And when I first saw Zanzibar town from the sea
It looked like the rich inner layers of an old conch
Fresh split in the light,
Reticulated, pink, peach, and white,
Here and there worn away into a strange shape
Or hidden by strings of sea moss, it lay
Between the jungle and the sea
That fell like shattered jewels
In very bright and varied blues
At its feet.

THE DESERT IN WINTER

It is the smell of sulphur
Coming up from under the earth in the heat
And the wet roots of dying reeds,
Half-slime, whose leaves cut
Like knife-blades when you
Run your hands over them. This is
The smell that brings it back.

A haze of sand over the sun—
Hardwoods in winter
The shiny greenish sunlight
On their stiff gray backs—
So that it seems to burn
distantly through thick glass,
an unaccountable moment of sadness.

This is the smell that brings it back,
A bubbling sulphur sludge,
Like rust ringed with rainbows,
That floats to the top of the desert spring,
The disturbance of water

Forcing its way through earth
That would otherwise be dead.
It forces its way up like a fist
Bringing yellow sulphur from the guts of the rocks

Red dragonflies scratch from the stems of the reeds
And a thousand colored birds hide in the dry thorn trees

MANGROVE SWAMP

I followed the sound of heavy wings,
The gliding underside of scaly feet
As they slipped into the water and knew
Where the Marabou storks were
Before I saw them,
Crouched together in the mangroves,
Unfolding their stiff red necks to see,
Clapping open the sided cones
Of their long gray jaws,
Like dull streaked plastic,
Hunched over a meal of marrow,
Carrion birds, gathered in the hills
Above the city at dusk. I found myself
Standing in a graveyard on a small hill,
On a path of upturned soil amid headstones
Cracked and overturned in the yellow grass
And below me were the mangrove swamps.
It was the hour before dark and the birds
were drawn to the slaughter house.
Its smell of cracked slippery bones and membranes
Just exposed to air, and the deep stirring
smell of blood begun to dry rose up to me
Where I stood. I walked
over hooves and horns dropped at random in the path
And had come stiff-shouldered and numb
Afraid as always of having been followed,
To see the city and the sea
from a distance at dusk.

Who like to show how
painful transformation is:
A man turning into a tree
Loses his fingers in leaves
His joints snap stiff, his skin
hangs loose in shag
He loses his eyes
To a new sense: wind
Water drawn up in his feet
feeds him and the dappled sun
thicks his blood to crystal

KINGFISHER AMONG THE TEACUPS

Would oh would I were a kingfisher—
That flies with the halcyons along the breaking waves,
with a fearless heart, that holy bird,
the deep blue of the sea

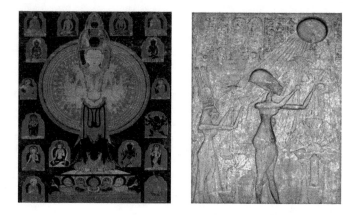

THE UNTRANSLATABLE WORD

The Cambridge classicist Jane Harrison wrote in 1912,
*Always pay attention to the untranslatable word, for there you may
rediscover the sanctity.*

To pursue an age-old question about an untranslatable
word:

What is the origin of the word Yahweh?

I offer an answer from my own observations: it is the hiero-
glyphic word **yahw**, the life-giving light that shines through all
things.

In the relief of Akhenaten the **yahw** hieroglyph, the
sun streaming light, gives life to plants and people on earth
alike. The rays of light are hands holding out the sign of life
to everything that lives. It is the image of Avalokiteshvara, *he
who looks down*, touching every living thing with a thousand
life-giving hands, open hands with eyes on them that see
all the suffering of the world, that they see the reality of the
world.

PART II

HEAVEN
IS A
WETLAND

and beyond them the mirrory river
full of forming stars

Sew green stones
The turquoise, malachite stars
And grow green
That Tety grow green
Green as a living reed

The soul is a jewel-like seed, planted in the glittering wetland
of the starry sky

*KER. Echoic Root, base of
various derivatives indicating
loud noises of birds.

(CRouk, Rook, Raven (koRax), cRow
cRane, shRiek, cRochet
cRack shRill zRash (kasvies)
cReak cuRlew (Rack, scReam)

'khaiRwan

کروان

and the cRane.

کرکی

κηξ

so, whose hooT-Q wet corner.
juT wiped out my list of birds.

Traya - pleiades
Sa2 - orion
lueizaim - sirius
Sahil - canopus

Atham (?)

Gidi (?)
Banat Naasi
Aqrab - scorpio

Kaichr - capella

hag - aunach

when Banat geer
fel & orion
& Banat Naasi -
Rain

when Bi Scorpion
fels in Moslem
month air from
- scorpion dit.
- bird but.

shoosh.
chi (seeds -
bright brown)

in times of no rain
they pick the seeds
of shoosh, the small
the chif & the grasses
his in the ground.
After they are dry
then they dig (digs)
pound them in.
flour & make
aside from here

Bedouin star names and shoosh — a desert plant eaten during
drought

THE COLORS OF STARS

Regulus flushed white
Arcturus yellow
Spica   brilliant white
Vega   sapphire blue
Antares red with emerald twin
Altair   yellow
Giedi   yellow
Matar
Fomalhaut   red
Aldeberan   pale rose
Al Nilam   bright white
Sirius   brilliant white

(stars rising Jan—Dec)
                all the winter stars are white
                    "no more than that yellow is green"

          *   *

        Green stars:
                Yildun, Zuben Esshemali
                Alcyone, Al Rescha
                Merak, Sadachbia

          *   *

*   *   *

Precious stones and metals, before they had any practical or monetary use, were valued because they captured a certain quality of light. Gold was the earthly guise of the sun god. The caps of the pyramids, stone falcons' wings overlaid were sheets of sunlight, as though a ray were caught and diffused right at one point, surrounding an object like a halo. So silver the moon. Gemstones recall the color of stars, but the colors of stars are alive, rose, sapphire, pale distant greens, the more conspicuous yellows (Arcturus the beryl star), the poisonous stars of Scorpio, red like the heat of summer.

Every ten days a new star group rose, and these decans were the foundation of star-clocks, and an early calendar, overlapping the cycles of the moon.

The perception of the stars as fields is still caught in *nejum*, the word for star in Arabic which in its plural form means also plants and flowers, from the verb najama, 'to appear'

The sky is called the Great Green; the plant Venus, Zuhra, is the Rose

THE SOUL BECOMES ORION

You are of the sky, born of twilight
You are of the sky with Orion
Who lives lives by gods' command,
and you live.

You rise with Orion in the eastern sky
And descend with Orion again in the west
The third with you is Sirius, purest of places,
Who leads you along the fair paths of the sky
Through fields of celestial rushes

You are of the sky - born of twilight

You rise of the sky with Orion

He who lives lives by god's command & you live!

You are born of dusk with Orion

You rise with Orion in the Eastern sky

And setting with Orion again in the west
The god with you is foremost - purest of places

He leads you along the fair paths of the sky

Through fields of celestial rushes

THE SOUL IS WASHED IN THE FIELD OF RUSHES, THE EASTERN STARS AT DAWN

Washed is he who is washed in the field of rushes
Washed is the light in the field of rushes
Washed is he who is washed in the field of rushes
Washed is Unis in the field of rushes

Unas lets Re lapis lazuli grow
Unas causes Re southern Sun P sprout

(plants + gems compared: growing in Re earth?)
also suggests lapis lazuli (blue stone)
grew in Egypt

275

(Re one)

THE SOUL BECOMES A WATERBIRD AND DANCES IN THE SKY

Observations on Hieroglyphic Birds in the Pyramid Texts

In the first verse on the north wall of the antechamber, the soul of the dead king flies up into the sky: on the right the verb pa, fly, is repeated papapa—a delightful onomatopoeic sound effect for a bird taking off from the water.

The word for waterbirds is apdu, spelled out in hieroglyphs and ending with three pictures of specific birds defining the word: the spur-winged goose, the widgeon, and the Eurasian spoonbill.

In the text that follows is the hieroglyphic verb "to dance" spelled out with the circle (ch) and the foot (b), chb, with the shrugging arms as the standard sign for the negative above it. What is the verb's determinative on the left—isn't it the foot of a waterbird taking off? Hence this is a verbal phrase presented as a charming hieroglyphic cartoon: does he not dance (in the sky)?

bird foot
human foot
⊙ — to dance

It has skin like Beni Adam but it is green, and it breathes like Beni Adam. Its eyes are gold, it has fingers and hands, it lives in sweet water, it comes out after rain and it sings all night long.

The verb to turn is an oryx

STAR
PRAYER
DAWN

The birds and the frogs of
Aristophanes — before, in nature words
Describing the world —
light words and animal
words — early description

msbb · Turn
(onyx)

to NYPL — so huge and warm
and comforting — in R.
Berg collection — letters
from R. poets. Lenny
wants to have time —
buy a farm and write.
How died the greatness
of writing — these letters
tell me.

Tale of — Refinnich
fedueir — his green blue eyes
and cropped white head.

of Oliver
Sedmani —
whose hair has
gone all white —
his bleached, light clear skin —

star (Sh.S.)

الغير   morning

morning. DAWN
morning star

Dws ntr · phosor
god

mз · onyx
pl.

mз hd ·
white onyx

h3h3 Ri stream

bright · white.
brightness ·
silver

Ri land

dreams cλred ·
bright T. dawn
(Ri shining
of Ri sun)

hзqw-šy
Bedouin- "Rise upon Ri
sead".

hnt šo 'upon
a lake'.
garden

NOTES

p. 4. Watching a thunderstorm come up on the seashore. *Something with rubbery round yellow leaves* is sea grape. The radiant love that receives all pain is *the great sea that surrounds us all.*

p. 6. *ariston men hudor* (Pindar, "Olympian 1," line 1).

p. 8. Three hieroglyphic words together in the dictionary: benighted traveler, hippopotamus, starry sky.

pp. 11, 14, 19. The poems "Zeitun," "Thaw," and "The Silver Forest" appeared in *Peripheries*, the poetry journal of Harvard Divinity School, in 2019.

p. 12. *The day that people are scattered over the earth like moths.* Like moths scattering in a thunderstorm. (From Sura 101 in the Quran, *The Day of Noise and Clamor.*)

p. 13. Pen-and-ink drawing of the garden at Andalusia on the Delaware. Translation of Mimnernus 13, 7th century BC.

p. 19. *The Silver Forest* is a conflation of four places. It is the realm of the dead in Homer. Nausicaa finds Odysseus passed out on a shore lined with poplar trees. A picnic on the shore of Lake Ontario drinking sherry under the silvery poplar trees with my mother and my great-aunt, the remarkable white sand shallows of the Great Lakes. On Stocking Island in the Exumas—a long empty stretch of seashore, divided from the harbor side by a silver forest of stunted seaside trees. My brother with his very blue eyes comes down the beach.

p. 20. Ezekiel 19:10.

pp. 20–21. Barweg and Eshar: two desert plants that grow in

the mist oasis of Gebel Elba on the Egypt-Sudan border.

p. 22. The lion as fire, the cow as water—who kills who? (From a Greek cenotaph in the Metropolitan Museum of Art.)

p. 24. Prehistoric rock drawings of cattle with trained horns from the Sahara.

p. 25. The Mahas tribe of North Sudan—their identifying scarring pattern is three deep vertical scars on each cheek. Lips are dyed blue with henna.

p. 26. Hollyhocks grow in the mist oasis of Elba.

p. 27. Iconographic reading of Andromeda: Andromeda is the female dragon Tiamat, the embodiment of chaos as the sea, the pure energy of the life force—chained/tamed by Perseus, *the destroyer*.

p. 28. In this beautiful fragment of Greek poetry from the 6th century BC, Ibycus 286 vividly captures the contrast of the seasons, with conception in marriage (spring) as a season. One thing that is very striking is his use of the word *parching*, that intense desire is *mania*, the Greek word for madness, and it is *thirst*. Pyasa is a Sanskrit word for thirst, a concept in Buddhism: that humankind is dying of the thirst of desire for things. Then there is the thirst for wisdom, for insight. Guru Dutt made this the title of his 1957 film about poetry: the longing of the poet, and the longing for the poet. As Emerson wrote in his essay *The Poet*, "On the brink of the waters of life and truth we are miserably dying."

p. 35. Describes a mangrove swamp in the Clove Islands.

p. 37. Ancient willow tree at the Dome of the Rock in Jerusalem.

p. 38. Translation of Alcman fragment 26. These lines (from a longer lost poetic work) were quoted by Antigonus. Alcman was a songwriter/choreographer working in Sparta in the seventh century BC, teaching his dances to bands of local girls to perform at seasonal festivals. His work survives in fragments, much of it discovered in a trash heap in Egypt in the early twentieth century.

p. 43. Pyramid of Tety. The soul is a jewel-like seed, planted in the glittering wetland of the starry sky.

p. 44. Bird notes from travels in the Eastern Desert with Joe Hobbs, co-author of *The Birds of Egypt* (Oxford University Press, 1989).

p. 53. From *The Names of Things*: bedouin description of a frog.

ABOUT THE AUTHOR

Susan Brind Morrow is the recipient of the Award in Literature from the American Academy of Arts and Sciences 2022. She is the author of *The Names of Things: A Passage in the Egyptian Desert, Wolves and Honey: A Hidden History of the Natural World*, and *The Dawning Moon of the Mind: Unlocking the Pyramid Texts*. Her work has appeared in *Harper's, The Nation, The Seneca Review, Peripheries: A Journal of Word and Image*, and *Lapham's Quarterly*. Morrow is currently at work on a book on darkness for Farrar, Straus and Giroux. Morrow is a former fellow of the Guggenheim Foundation and a fellow of the New York Institute of the Humanities, and an author whose papers are in The Sowell Family Collection of Literature, Community and the Natural World.